Original title:
Blooming Indoors

Copyright © 2025 Creative Arts Management OÜ
All rights reserved.

Author: Ryan Sterling
ISBN HARDBACK: 978-1-80581-767-3
ISBN PAPERBACK: 978-1-80581-294-4
ISBN EBOOK: 978-1-80581-767-3

## Quiet Corners

In the shadow of the shelf,
A cactus waves, saying 'help!'
It guards the dust bunnies' flight,
And claims the couch for its night.

## **Loud Colors**

Pink polka dots and lime twist,
A party in the air, not missed!
The curtains wink, the carpets cheer,
Cupcakes for flowers, oh dear, oh dear!

## Whispering Petals of the Hearth

A pot of violets starts to giggle,
As they share secrets, dance, and wiggle.
The fern nearby gives side-eye glances,
For it won't join in any of those dances.

## **Rebirth in a Vase**

Roses on a diet, they swore to shed,
Watered with soda, they're feeling quite red.
Tulips sport shades of rainbow delight,
Wishing they'd remember their manners, polite!

## **Indoor Wildflowers**

When daisies demand a sunflower hat,
And the pansies try to chat with the cat,
The thrill of the wind jumping through the door,
Turns every room into a garden galore!

## The Calmness of Ferns

In a pot all snug and neat,
The ferns play hide and seek,
Whispering secrets to the sun,
Their laughter's never bleak.

A spider lurks, but he's quite shy,
Waving leaves, oh me, oh my!
Ferns roll their eyes, don't make a fuss,
In their leafy world, they just trust.

Morning light brings them such cheer,
They dance with joy, we hold our beer!
Their fronds a show, a leafy spree,
Who needs a dance floor? Just look and see!

So next time you tread with foot so light,
Tiptoe past this green delight,
For in this pot, there's peace and glee,
Ferns laugh it off, as if to say, "We're free!"

## **Enclosed Harmony in Fragrant Clouds**

In a jar, the basil grows tall,
Swaying gently with the call,
Of every meal that's yet to form,
It dreams of pesto in a storm.

Mint's got jokes, and oh so sly,
Whispers tales of pie in the sky,
While parsley rolls its funny eyes,
Declaring competitions with surprise.

The rosemary sings a deep ballad,
As thyme comes in with quick salad,
Together in the window's light,
They giggle at the chef's delight.

In this little cozy space,
Herbs find joy—let's party, ace!
With aromas strong and sweet,
Who knew plants could be so neat?

So here's to greens in jars so bright,
Creating laughter day and night,
In their world of fragrant dreams,
Life's a joke—so it seems!

## Whispers of the Potted Heart

My cactus speaks in prickled tones,
It jabbers on through rusty moans.
"Water me more, I need a sip!"
While I just smile, tight-lipped.

The fern pretends it's oh so grand,
With leaves like fans, it takes a stand.
It sways and bends, a leafy tease,
But dust gathers like frozen breeze.

## Petals in the Corner

There's a rogue plant in the corner wide,
It claims it's an exotic pride.
But all it does is droop and pout,
A floral diva with no clout.

A sunflower laughs, its height so bold,
"From the pot, you'll never unfold!"
Yet it wilts when the wind blows strong,
Poking at the petals all day long.

**Sunlit Secrets of the Windowsill**

The sun pokes in, a cheeky guest,
Whispering tales of planty zest.
"Open wide, let those leaves stretch!"
While dust bunnies huddle, quite fetched.

A basil plant dreams of Italian air,
"Pasta!" it sighs, with fragrant flair.
While thyme just chuckles, "What a tease,
A herb that daydreams, oh please!"

## The Dance of Indoor Flora

The pot of daisies giggles and sways,
"Let's have a party! Dance all day!"
They twirl and spin on a saucer base,
Hoping the cat won't join the race.

A violet blushes, "Look at me!"
"Not so bright," the marigold will decree.
Together they pot-luck with glee,
Chasing each other to the nearby pea.

## Sunlit Refuge

In the corner, a pot sits tight,
Leaves performing a dance, oh what a sight!
A cactus wearing a cowboy hat,
Brother to the fern who thinks he's a brat.

A sly little spider, weaving with flair,
Tries to tickle the peace lily's hair.
The cat looks puzzled, with a raised brow,
As he tiptoes softly—what happened, how?

## Life Beyond the Windowpane

A bird pecks at glass, thinking it's food,
While inside my plant does the latest mood.
Swaying like dancers in a wild rave,
As I paint their leaves with a coffee wave.

The sun sneezes rays, oh what a show,
While my thyme whispers secrets to the aglow.
An earwig's auditioning, quite the charmer,
I give him a round of applause, "You're a farmer!"

**Lush Hues in Stilled Air**

The pothos climbs like a cheeky lad,
Searching for light—oh my, what a fad!
Cacti with arms raised in mid-salute,
And a rubber plant singing, "Ain't I cute?"

When the vacuum hums, it's a dance-off time,
With dirt on the floor, it's almost a crime.
The orchids giggle when no one can hear,
Over spiced tea, life's a delight, never fear!

## The Art of Indoor Eden

My basil's a chef, dreaming of fame,
While the mint tells stories of sweet candy game.
The dracaena thinks it's a runway show,
Winking at the sun like it's in the know.

When I spill some water, the aloe just grins,
"More moisture, please, let the party begin!"
A mix of wildness, it's a colorful fuss,
In this tiny jungle, life's ridiculous.

**Radiance Behind Closed Doors**

In the corner, a cactus pricks,
Cheering on the love for tricks.
Little daisies dance with flair,
Chasing socks that vanish in air.

Window sills, a wild parade,
Pots of basil in bright charade.
A fern in shades, all mixed and fun,
Sipping sunlight, just begun.

Mismatched mugs hold secrets deep,
While rubber plants in silence creep.
Turns out, the geranium's a spy,
Listening to our laughter fly.

So let's toast with soil and joy,
To every plant, each leaf their ploy.
Who knew a home could giggle so?
Where every potted friend steals the show?

## The Quiet Revolution of Leaves

A succulent stood up one day,
Declared 'I'm here to spice the fray.'
With a wink and a leafy cheer,
It took the room and made it clear.

Potting soil turned into a soap,
As a spider plant swang from hope.
In every corner laughter grew,
With every petal, a joke or two.

The peace lily wore a crown of pride,
As a rubber tree tried to hide.
Such leafy rebels, on display,
Taking naps in a sunbeam play.

Envy simmered in the air,
As daisies giggled without a care.
In this quiet, leafy clout,
We found the joy that sprouted out.

## Rewilding the Interior

Oh look! A pothos swings and twirls,
While my cat plots to cause some swirls.
The cardboard box is now a den,
For wondering squirrels, oh where have you been?

A jungle grows with clothes in heaps,
And cheeky vines that climb and peep.
Shoes converted into a plant's throne,
In this madness, who feels alone?

My rosemary wears a tiny hat,
As the sunflowers spin—how 'bout that?
Each herb has tales, their own delight,
Who needs a farm when it's all in sight?

So come for tea with the happy greens,
Where ferns are kings and joy convenes.
Let's throw a party, pots all around,
In this wild interior, happiness found.

## Kaleidoscope of In-House Blossoms

Lily pads on cushions bloom,
Imparting cheer in every room.
The violets giggle, quite refined,
As candles flicker, leaving behind.

Petunias grow, gossiping fast,
While ferns roll dice for a playful cast.
Each bedside, an escapade so bright,
Cactus costumes just feel right.

Floral patterns twirl and spin,
As roses act like they're all in.
Twirling in their vibrant dance,
Who knew flora could take a chance?

So fill your home with laughter's lift,
Each petal shares a winking gift.
In this magical, colorful spree,
Let's celebrate our leafed jubilee.

## Nature's Sanctuary Under Glass

In a pot, a cactus sighs,
Wishing it could roam the skies.
The fern just dances, never still,
While I chase dust with great goodwill.

The spider plant, oh what a tale,
It thinks it's on a leafy scale.
Caught in the sun's warm embrace,
That little guy still claims the space.

## Sunkissed Corners

Sunbeams bounce from wall to wall,
My plants engage in a bright brawl.
The pothos laughs, hanging low,
While the rubber plant steals the show.

A succulent poses with such pride,
With little green arms open wide.
The peace lily rolls its eyes in glee,
'Look at me, the royalty!'

## A Symphony of Leaves

In the corner, a monster smiles,
While I rearrange it for a while.
A symphony of greens and shades,
As I dance through my leafy glades.

The dracaena hums a tune,
While basking under the afternoon.
The sage starts to crack jokes galore,
And I can't help but laugh some more.

## Vibrant Hues in Small Spaces


In tiny pots, colors collide,
As I clip another leaf with pride.
A rainbow of petals, such a sight,
Who knew chaos could feel so right?

The violets giggle in their row,
Complaining that they need to grow.
While herbs share gossip, rich and sage,
Turning my home into a stage!

## **Echoes of Spring Inside**

A cactus wears a tiny hat,
With bright flowers on his mat.
The geraniums shake, dance, and twirl,
While the ivy chats with the pearl.

My cat thinks they're a buffet feast,
But the plants just laugh, to say the least.
The fern's a fan of a good joke,
But the rubber tree's gone all rogue!

**Petal-Scented Air**

In a room where daisies sing,
Bees buzz in, doing their thing.
Socks hiding under the potted peas,
Who knew plants had such funky degrees!

A sunflower's grinning with delight,
Petals like disco balls in the light.
Who knew plants had such a sense of style?
They throw parties; stay awhile!

## The Green Oasis Within

The leaves whisper secrets so sly,
While I sip tea and just watch them fly.
A bonsai's contemplating its height,
While the orchids hold a mock fight.

Succulents giggle, "Look at us shine!"
As I trip on stray vines; oh how divine!
The aloe's giving a spa day treat,
By the end, I'm not on my feet!

## Nature's Courtyard at Home

Inside my house, the daisies race,
They think they can win in a silly chase.
The phalaenopsis pirouettes around,
While the potted herbs just stand their ground.

A tiny ant plays peek-a-boo,
The peonies gossip; oh, it's true!
In this courtyard where laughter is free,
Even plants know how to be silly with glee!

## Inside the Garden's Embrace

In a pot sits a cactus, all spiky and tough,
It swears it can dance, yet can't move a fluff.
The fern claims it's shy, hides under a leaf,
While the sunflowers giggle, beyond disbelief.

The old bonsai grumbles, 'I used to be tall!'
It sips tea with succulents and never feels small.
A tiny green spider, a guest for some cheer,
Calls out, 'Who needs sunlight? I shine always here!'

## The Pulse of Potted Dreams

A basil plant mutters, 'I'm dying to bake!'
While thyme rolls its eyes, 'Come on, what's at stake?'
Down by the window, the parsley is spry,
It croons to the air, 'Oh, how time flies by!'

The geranium sneezes, says, 'I've got the flu!'
But all of the roses just giggle, 'Achoo!'
The potting shed's buzzing with laughter and tea,
As the potted dreams jive with glee, can't you see?

## Nurtured in Shadows

In the corner, a shadow with secrets to share,
A vine whispers softly, 'Hey, I'm still here!'
The pothos is plotting to reach for the light,
While the spider plant schemes, 'I could be quite bright!'

The peace lily sighs, 'I prefer midnight chats,'
While ferns roll their fronds and say, 'How about that?'
'We thrive in the dark, it's a cozy affair,
Spreading our love, like we just don't care!'

## Fragments of Flora

Twirling in pots, each a character bold,
The violets gossip, 'Did you hear? She's sold!'
An orchid looks scandalous, dressed up in style,
Boasting of petals, it's been here a while.

The lavender dreams of a dance with the bees,
While daisies just chill, sipping dew like teas.
'It's a riot,' they sing, 'in our little space,'
Flowers of humor, a whimsical place!

## Serenity in Soil

In a pot sits a cactus, looking quite mad,
Complainst about sunlight, says it's just bad.
The fern does the tango, so lush and so green,
While my sad little basil just wishes to preen.

Oh, the thyme is a thinker, plotting its day,
While mint in the corner just chews on some hay.
We laugh at the petals, that dance with pure glee,
'You can't see our roots, but they're wild as can be!'

## A Memento of Nature's Hand

Got a plant that's named Larry, he's quite the celeb,
Lights up the whole room with his green, leafy web.
He's got jokes in his leaves, oh, can he delight,
Makes the pothos giggle all day and all night.

A cactus named Spike, in the corner does sit,
Says he's got prickles, but he's really a hit.
While roses just blush and throw petals around,
Whispering secrets that barely make sound.

## **Shadows of the Botanical**

The snake plant is silent, a true introvert,
While the violets gossip and wear all their flirt.
The orchids, so fancy, sip tea from a cup,
And all of their antics, I just can't keep up!

The aloe's a hero, heals cuts on the fly,
But with all his sharp features, he's still quite the guy.
Jade plant is hoarding coins, oh what a sight,
You'd think he's investing in stocks overnight!

## The Flourishing Heart of Home

In my cozy corner, green friends all reside,
Chasing away blues, oh what a wild ride!
The ivy is creeping and making a spree,
Challenging all to join in the jubilee!

The peace lily winks, says she's holding a show,
While the bamboo insists that it's growing, you know.
We twirl in the sunlight, in laughter and cheer,
Picking up potting soil, year after year!

## Tending to the Quiet

In pots that dance on windowsills,
The herbs debate their garden skills.
With mint that claims its rightful space,
And basil's serious, wrinkled face.

The soil whispers, 'You're too loud!'
While succulents form a leafy crowd.
Each plant a superstar, no doubt,
As houseplants plot to take the route!

## **Serenity Among Stems**

A cactus jabs at morning light,
While ferns swoon in a leafy fright.
Pansies laugh at how they'll shine,
As petals sip on sunlight wine.

A tangled vine starts to cascade,
While orchids flaunt their colorful parade.
The rosemary plots a fragrant scheme,
In this indoor plant-based dream!

**Rebirth Under the Roof**


The wilting leaves had quite the show,
But now they're back with vibrant glow.
Forgotten pots now full of cheer,
As plants declare, 'We're still right here!'

With watering cans like royal crowns,
And dirt that falls, it frolics down.
The spider plant gets tangled in,
As laughter bursts — let the fun begin!

## Lush Life in Small Places

On top of shelves, a jungle thrives,
With sneaky roots that twist and jive.
A pothos peeks around the bend,
While ferns insist they like to blend.

When sunlight hits, they sway with glee,
And whisper secrets, oh so free.
A life confined, yet wild and bold,
In quirky pots with stories told!

## A Garden in Glass

Windows dressed in green, so spry,
Plants in pots reach for the sky.
They wave their leaves, a leafy cheer,
While I water them, spill some beer.

Cacti frown, they know my clums,
While orchids dance, ignoring hums.
The fern finds space for a tiny hat,
Unbothered by the clanging cat.

Sunflowers stretch with all their might,
Yet, in their pots, they can't take flight.
A spider plant laughs and sways,
As it tricks me with its leafy ways.

In here, life's a leafy spree,
Where pots and laughter grow with glee.
Each sprout and stem, a comic show,
Who knew plants could steal the glow?

## The Language of Leaves

Whispers rustle in the night,
As leaves converse with pure delight.
They gossip 'bout the sun's new glare,
While I sit in my rumpled chair.

"Did you see that bug? No, the other one!"
"Watch out! The cat's about to run!"
Branches giggle, twigs exchange,
Their leafy chat is quite the range.

The pothos laughs, "I'm growing wild,"
While succulents act like a shy child.
A peace lily rolls its eyes quite grand,
At the moss that just can't understand.

So here we sit, a green parade,
Where silly tales will never fade.
My plants are wise, I must confess,
Who needs a book when you can bless?

## Radiance in the Shadows

In the corner, shadows creep,
While plants awake from cozy sleep.
Little sunbeams peek and pose,
Brightening up these leafy shows.

The rubber tree shines, oh so proud,
Contrived like it's a beauty crowd.
A wandering Jew, with flair so bold,
Keeps talking back, defying cold.

The calathea spins, a dance divine,
As dust bunnies start to entwine.
They're sharing secrets, it seems quite loud,
Muffled laughter among the proud.

What a circus thrives today,
In shadows where the sillies play!
With radiance bright, they all rejoice,
Who knew in silence, they'd find their voice?

## Solitary Petals

One lone petal, left to sigh,
In a room where colors fly.
"Why am I here, all alone?"
Asked the flower with a fidgety tone.

"Everyone's dancing, moving about,
While I sit here, looking out."
Her neighbors twirl, what a sight,
But she remains, not feeling right.

Then she hatches quite a scheme,
To start a party, a leafy dream.
With a twirl and a flutter, she shouts with glee,
"Come join my party, you leaves, so free!"

Suddenly, she feels the love,
As petals gather from above.
No longer solitary in her plight,
Her laughter fills the room tonight!

## Greenery's Embrace

In the corner, a fern does dance,
Poking fun, it takes a chance.
Whispering leaves with playful prance,
Who knew plants could throw a glance?

Potted pals in ceramic suits,
Throwing shade like sneaky brutes.
They giggle in their leafy roots,
Chasing dust like playful hoots.

## Nature's Soft Murmur

A cactus flaunts its prickly pride,
In the sunlight, it likes to hide.
Throwing jokes like spiky tide,
"Who needs friends?" it teases wide.

The herbs in pots are quite the crew,
Counting leaves, as they often do.
"Basil's winning!" says parsley too,
While mint just giggles, "I'm so cool!"

## Echoes of Growth Inside

In the kitchen, the ivy sprawls,
Climbing high and having balls.
Chasing sunlight as it calls,
"Can't catch me!" it proudly sprawls.

The orchids strut in regal wear,
Throwing stares without a care.
"Who's the fairest?" they declare,
"Watch us blossom, come and stare!"

## Colors in Confinement

Pansies giggle, a vibrant jest,
Daring sunbeams, they're the best.
"Can't touch this!" they jest with zest,
In windowsills, they love to rest.

Bamboo buddies grow tall and sly,
Peeking over with a wink and sigh.
"Bet you wish you could fly high!"
They whisper secrets, oh my my!

## **Heartbeats of Foliage**

In the corner, green friends sway,
With wild dreams of sunshine play.
They whisper jokes to the old vase,
As dust bunnies laugh in their space.

A fern thinks it's a great tree,
While succulents giggle with glee.
The spider plant flirts with the light,
Convinced it's a star, oh what a sight!

Pothos is plotting to climb the wall,
While cacti wonder if they're too small.
In a world where they can't go out,
Their tiny hearts still dance about.

One leaf has a crush on the cat,
But it knows it's in a love spat.
With every petal, they share a grin,
In this quirky room, life's a win!

## **Flourish in Closed Quarters**

A rubber plant wears a new hat,
Cushioned by pillows, look at that!
Each leaf steals a moment to cheer,
Even while trapped, they find good cheer.

The basil dreams of a pizza slice,
While the mint teases, 'Mine's more nice!'
A tiny thyme shouts, 'I'm the spice!'
They giggle at fates, making life twice.

In the darkness, they pull a prank,
And wear wacky faces on the flank.
With soil beneath and roots that play,
They turn this home into cabaret!

Oh, the mischief of plants combined,
With jokes and jests, they're unconfined.
Growing wild in this indoor land,
With potting soil and nursing hands.

## Captured Essence of Flora

A tiny seed dreams of the sky,
In its pot, it can only sigh.
Chatting herbs plot their escape,
While daisies dress up in bright drape.

Oh, the orchids tease each other so,
With tales of places they won't go.
'We could be queens in a garden fair,'
But they're happy in this comfy lair.

The African violets make a scene,
Acting like they're in a magazine.
With dramatic poses and winks so sly,
They know it's fab with a small alibi.

A snake plant gives a gentle grin,
Saying, 'We're fabulous; let's begin!'
In their pots with a dash of flair,
They're the best comedy show anywhere!

## Hushed Murmurs From the Soil


In the dark, the roots start to chat,
Sharing secrets, a gossip spree, just like that!
A rumor bursts: 'Have you seen—'
How the potting mix can get so clean?

The cactus brags about its fluff,
Saying, 'I'm sturdy, I've got the stuff!'
While ferns counter, 'We're graceful and green!'
Together they laugh like a lively scene.

Dirt piles up on the windowsill,
As petals plan a takeoff thrill.
They mimic the rustle of the breeze,
While plotting adventures with perfect ease.

In this confined pocket of cheer,
These leafy whispers can't help but appear.
Though sheltered away from the vast outside,
They keep the laughter alive, full of pride.

## **The Indoor Eden**

In pots they sit, a leafy crew,
With a quirky smile, they tease me too.
Like little dancers in a sunny sprawl,
I trip over them, oh what a fall!

Their green thumbs up, they cheer me on,
As I pretend my chores are gone.
A dandelion's wish, but more refined,
They whisper secrets of a joyful kind.

Each morning's brew, I spill in haste,
They gawk, they giggle, at my clumsy taste.
With every petal, laughter rises,
These plants, my friends, come with surprises!

In an indoor heaven, chaos blooms,
Between the sunshine and flavorful fumes.
Not just decor, they play their part,
In this wacky, green-filled work of art!

## Nature's Refuge

Here they are, my leafy kin,
Taking bets on what's a win.
With sun in their eyes, they cheer and sway,
While I chase the dust bunnies away!

Cactus with arms, say "Give us a hug!"
While herbs conspire for a culinary rug.
I trip on a fern, what a scene!
These plants are wild, if you know what I mean!

The IV drip of watering cans,
Turns me into quite the frantic fan.
Greens giggle as I dance around,
In my little jungle, chaos is found!

Pothos hangs low, just like my mood,
But laughs out loud, as I'm in a food feud.
With roots so deep, they've got the scoop,
In this indoor base, we form a troupe!

## Quiet Burst of Life

In corners wide, with thrift-store lamps,
The plants all plot their leafy camps.
A neighbor's cat, too curious, peeks,
As greenery giggles, my heart it tweaks.

Each petal's wink, a gentle tease,
While I do battle with the dust and sneeze.
The seedlings laugh at my clumsy care,
As they sprout dreams, unaware I'm there!

Tiny buds pop open with glee,
In viney antics, they're wild and free.
I join the party, dancing with glee,
While soil flings itself right at me!

A window's edge, hosting glee so bright,
Tiny limbs reaching, dreams taking flight.
Together we laugh, in our messy nest,
As an indoor world feels truly blessed!

## Tender Tendrils of Joy

With a pot of soil, my home's alive,
Where tiny sprouts of humor thrive.
Tendrils snake around every chair,
Offering comfort, a green affair.

Their whispers echo in the air,
With puns and jokes, they make me care.
As I water them, they giggle and gleam,
Turns out the plants, they all dream!

In the morning sun, we plan and plot,
As leaves up high say, "Gotcha, hotshot!"
A thimble of sunshine begins the show,
As they twist and twine, stealing the glow.

In my quirky abode, they rule the scene,
These leafy pals, all lush and green.
With smiles and roots, our stories blend,
In this tangle of life, we're all best friends!

## Sheltered Spirituality

In the corner, a plant takes a snooze,
Dreaming of sun and the outside blues.
With a tiny leaf, it waves goodbye,
Hoping one day it'll touch the sky.

Dust bunnies dance on the windowsill,
While my cactus gives off a prickly thrill.
Sipping my tea, I watch in delight,
Who knew houseplants could put up such a fight?

With a gentle nudge, I give a cheer,
"Grow tall, my friend, have no fear!"
Stuck here with me, it's a sad plight,
Yet it holds its ground, a true delight.

Though we're indoors, our spirits are high,
Who needs sunshine? We've got this pie!
Yoga with ferns, a cozy retreat,
Life's funny when nature brings the heat!

# Beauty Beneath the Ceiling

Above my head, a fern goes wild,
Every inch a new foliage child.
The shadows dance with a soft embrace,
While dust collects in a top secret place.

A pot of violets plots a scheme,
To steal the sunlight, oh what a dream!
They whisper secrets to my favorite chair,
Telling tall tales of a world unfair.

The hamster's wheeling, the cat's on patrol,
As my leafy friends make their way to a goal.
Who needs the garden when joy runs high,
With ferns and silliness under the sky?

So here I sit with my gang of green,
In a funny world, where we're all seen.
Together we thrive, in this indoor scene,
Adding laughter and joy to the mundane routine.

## Growing Hope in Solitude

In the quiet corners, a little sprout,
Wonders what this indoor life's about.
Its leaves flutter like they're on parade,
While I applaud from my comfy shade.

A stray sock becomes a cozy nest,
For a wandering rogue in search of rest.
Each petal a laugh in a solemn house,
Filling the space, I cheer and douse.

Mismatched pots tell incomplete tales,
Of voyages lost on indoor trails.
Sunbeams slip through like mischievous friends,
Sharing smiles like they're on the mend.

We share a giggle by the fridge so near,
"Let's grow together, have no fear!"
In solitude's glow, we dance and sway,
In this funny saga, we find our way.

## Captivated by Chlorophyll

In the kitchen, a basil plant asserts,
"Chop me up and serve with shirts!"
It stretches wide as if to mock,
The herbs that dare to take stock.

A rubbery fern, with attitude strong,
Wiggles and jiggles all day long.
"Move over, spider plant, I need that light!"
They battle for space in leafy delight.

The sunlight trickles, like jokes in the air,
Hydrangeas giggle without a care.
Together we flourish, in dumbfound glee,
Creating a circus of greenery spree.

So here we sit, where the laughter flows,
In pots of delight, a symphony grows.
As chlorophyll laughs, and I sip my tea,
Life's a funny garden, come laugh with me!

## Curling Vines of Comfort

In corners they twist and play,
Chasing sunlight all the day.
Monstera's making quite the mess,
While spider plants create distress.

They gather dust and gossip too,
Who knew they had so much to do?
A leaf that tickles, oh what fun,
I swear they're plotting, just for fun!

Each tendril stretches with a laugh,
Plotting a new growth photograph.
I hear them whisper, 'Look at me!',
Competing for the best selfie.

With pots as thrones, they sit and stare,
As if they own the whole dang air.
Green royalty, they take their turns,
While I water, my patience burns.

## Whispers of Greenery

Silly succulents stretch their backs,
Dreaming of deserts and relaxing hacks.
Pothos grins in a leafy spree,
As if they know the secret key.

Ferns flap their fronds in a merry dance,
Each one hoping for a glance.
They giggle softly under the light,
'This isn't bad, we'll stay the night!'

Cacti boast of their prickly pride,
'We're the tough ones,' they provide.
Yet when it rains, they hide like fools,
Just keeping up with all the rules.

A dance party in the living room,
Each plant a wedged blossom's plume.
With pots like bowls, they sing with glee,
Just leaf it to them, they'll agree!

## The Secret Life of Houseplants

When night falls, they throw a shindig,
A wild affair, is it too big?
Hiding in shadows, they prance around,
With dance floors made of soil, unbound.

LED lights spark a funky scene,
Where rubber plants become the queens.
The bamboo flutes play soft and low,
Imagining beds of tinsel and glow.

Philodendrons do the twist and twirl,
While orchids in tutus give a whirl.
Each sprout with dreams of a grand stage,
Strutting 'cross the carpet like a sage.

'No humans allowed!' they bravely state,
In their leafy robes, they celebrate.
While I sit and sip my tea,
Unaware of their silly spree.

## **Petals in the Living Room**


Daisies plop on the coffee table,
Plotting schemes like trusty fables.
While geraniums trade the news,
In vibrant hues and cheeky views.

Tulips gossip, their heads held high,
'Tell me, have you seen the sky?'
While violets dance and roll about,
Chasing dust bunnies, there's no doubt.

In this flower power retreat,
They sip on dew, a tasty treat.
With every petal's secret sway,
They share the laughs from day to day.

So if you're feeling drab and gray,
Just peek at them, bright as May!
For petals know the art of cheer,
In every room, they're always near.

## Senses Awakened by Leaves

In a pot, my fern did sway,
It mimics dance in its own way.
Who knew that dirt could smell so sweet?
With every sprout, a little treat.

The spider plant has taken charge,
It thinks it's grown to be quite large.
Swinging leaves like they're on a spree,
Is it a plant or a circus with glee?

Tiny blooms on ledges peek,
As if to say, "Come on, take a sneak!"
With petals soft and colors bright,
Desire for sunlight, what a plight!

Yet here I sit, my tea in hand,
Listening to the green life stand.
Each rustle brings a giggle near,
My leafy pals, I hold you dear.

## Cupped Petals of Serenity

On the shelf, a cup of color,
With petals bright, it attracts a holler.
Jasmine giggles with a fragrance sweet,
Whispers of nature in a cozy seat.

A cactus waves with prickly cheer,
"I won't bite, just come right here!"
It tells the jokes of desert sun,
"What's green and a clown? Just wait for fun!"

Violets gossip in pastel hues,
In their debate, they take their views.
"Who's the fairest?" one leaf cries,
They'll never vote, they're quite the wise!

Through the window, they soak up light,
Chasing shadows, what a sight!
Inside this jungle of color and glee,
I sip my tea, laughing quietly.

## Gentle Giants of the Sunroom

In my sunroom, giants grow tall,
With leafy arms that brush the wall.
"Watch your head!" they call with cheer,
These plants are large, but hearts sincere.

A rubber tree plays peek-a-boo,
Its glossy leaves a stunning view.
"I can stretch!" it claims with pride,
As I duck low, trying to hide.

A monstera plots its next big feat,
"What flavor am I? A tasty treat?"
Its holes like smiles, oh what a grin,
Each new leaf is where fun begins.

But giants need space, that is a fact,
To strut their stuff, they'll never act.
A dance-off? Bring it on, my friends,
In this sunroom, the fun never ends!

## Nature's Soliloquy

In the corner, a solo bloom,
Singing sweetly, chasing gloom.
"I'm so fabulous, can't you see?"
It sways and swirls, as proud as can be.

A busy bee flits here and there,
"I'm on important pollen air!"
It buzzes loudly, like it's fame,
Nature's dance is quite the game.

Leaves whisper secrets with a rustle,
"Come closer, we've got a hustle!"
They chime in with giggles and sneezes,
A merry chaos sprouting breezes.

From tiny pots, the symphony grows,
With each new sprout, the laughter flows.
Nature's charm in a playful art,
In every leaf, a joyful heart.

## Lush Life in Tidy Spaces

In a pot on the windowsill,
A tiny sprout does thrill.
It waves its leaves to the sun,
Saying, "I'm the chosen one!"

Watering can, I'm not a mom,
Just here to play the calm,
My plants think I'm quite a clown,
They giggle when I talk them down.

A cactus with a prickly grin,
Tells me, "I'm the king within!"
I tried to give it a hug,
Now it's stuck like a bug!

In my house, we're all quite snug,
Plants gossip while I jug.
Chasing sunlight, what a tease,
They're growing tall with such ease!

# Flora's Embrace in Closed Walls

On my shelf sit petunias bright,
Chatting with violets every night.
They squabble over who's more cute,
As I laugh in my oversized boot.

Air plants are swinging, feeling free,
Dancing to tunes sung by me.
"Don't cling too tight," I often say,
"Or I'll forget to water you today!"

Sunlight's peeking through the glass,
Promising growth, and a bit of sass.
My fiddle leaf starts to sway,
Knowing it won't see the fray.

With soil on my shoes, I step,
In my garden, secrets kept.
Every day, I watch them reach,
For the laughing light they beseech!

## Rejuvenation in Planter's Light

In a corner where the sun's been told,
I've got herbs that are brave and bold.
Basil's whispering, "Add some spice!"
While parsley's asking for a nice slice.

I talk to my succulents at dawn,
Wishing them luck during the yawn.
They roll their eyes, oh what a crew,
Knowing they're too cool for the dew.

My fern's got flair—a frilly do,
Checking the mirror, "How do I look to you?"
I nod and say, "Quite stylish, dear!"
Knowing it's the plants I hold dear.

Everyone's vying for center stage,
In this indoor leafy cage.
I might be the one pulling strings,
But they're the true plant-based kings!

## Gentle Growth in a Glass Shelter

In my terrarium, the world's so neat,
Mini-ecosystem, what a treat!
Beetles and moss with their silly ways,
Keep me chuckling through my days.

Tiny worlds behind glass walls,
Where even the smallest leaf recalls,
That life is a game of hide and seek,
With shadows hiding both strong and weak.

Lettuce is lounging, carrots tease,
Saying, "We grow with so much ease!"
While beans throw shade, quite literally,
Hoping to take the throne eventually.

In this quirky, cluttered nook,
Every plant's got its own book.
Tales of sunshine, rain, and fun,
Together they bask, my green army won!

**Hidden Petals of Home**

In a sock drawer, green thumb's delight,
Plants sprouting, oh what a sight!
Cacti wearing socks on their spines,
Saying, 'Hey there, I'm doing just fine!'

Kitchen cabinet, a leafy surprise,
Herbs laughing, 'We're foodies in disguise!'
Basil plays chef, with parsley in tow,
Cooking up mischief wherever they grow.

Potted peas peek from behind the chair,
Giggles float in the summer air.
'Are we veggies?', they ask with glee,
Just wait till dinner, wait and see!

A fern in the bathroom, oh what a scene,
Happily soaking in the steam like a queen.
Toilet roles in a flower pot stand,
"Oh well," says the plant, "Life's simply grand!"

## Flourishing in the Edges

On the windowsill, a tiny parade,
Succulents dancing in bright lemonade.
One tried to salsa, but slipped on a leaf,
Now he's just rooting for applause, not grief!

The snail took a stroll, oh what a joke,
While the pothos said, 'I'm not a cloak!'
Hanging around, in a sad sack way,
'Please attach me to something today!'

The spider plant thinks it's a star,
Swinging its tendrils, saying, 'Look how far!'
And I say, 'Not too much, please hold on tight,'
Or else we might end up in a green fight!

One little vine is planning a heist,
Stealing the sunlight, oh isn't that nice?
"Come join the fun!" whispers the pot,
Together we'll flourish, oh why not a lot?"

## Garden Magic Under a Roof

The ceiling fan spins, it's a garden in flight,
With fake vines that think they're the real light.
'We're as alive as this dusty shelf,'
Chuckles the fern, 'Don't judge by yourself!'

A sunflower peeks from behind the couch,
Practicing how not to be a slouch.
'With seeds of laughter, I'll grow tall and bright,
Just need a little sun and the couch won't bite!'

The cat thinks he's king of this green domain,
Prowling past planters, declaring his reign.
But every flower shrieks with delight,
"Beware of the furball, it's quite a fright!"

The breadbasket sprouts with herbiness so bold,
Where once was a loaf, a jungle now unfolds.
'Got breadsticks?' laughs the basil on high,
With humor like this, we'll always get by!

## **Roots Beneath the Surface**

Under the floorboards, a secret convention,
Roots hold meetings with utmost intention.
"I'll grow to the kitchen," one said with a grin,
"Let's see who gets watered, let the games begin!"

A lettuce leaf's plotting a leap for the sky,
While radishes chuckle, "Give it a try!"
"Sure, let's get outside!" said a spunky sweet pea,
"Free snacks from a picnic, let's all agree!"

The soil whispers tales of underground wars,
"Watch out for the mop, it's claiming our doors!
But with dirt on our side and roots like a dream,
We'll conquer this house, or so it would seem!"

So here we sprout, in pots and in planters,
Making a ruckus as leafy infiltrators.
For in every corner, with giggles and cheer,
We're the homegrown wonders, loud and clear!

**Embracing Growth in Four Walls**

In my little box of cheer,
Plants dance without any fear.
Chasing sunlight's warm embrace,
While I'm stuck in this tight space.

A cactus waves its tiny hands,
Demanding water like it's planned.
Herbs plotting culinary schemes,
As I daydream with delusional dreams.

Ferns whisper secrets to the air,
While dust bunnies act like they care.
Succulents giggle with their spines,
Turning my home into a jungle of vines.

So here we are, a quirky crew,
Green pals in this indoor zoo.
Trading stories, growing tall,
Who needs the outdoors at all?

## Nature's Whisper in Every Room

In my kitchen, sprigs of thyme,
Claiming they taste just like a dime.
They argue with the garlic bread,
As I shift my eyes and nod my head.

A fern hangs low, like it's pouting,
As if to say, 'Keep that shouting!'
While a rubber plant gives a wink,
I question if they ever drink.

The ivy creeps up on my lamp,
Pretending to be a little tramp.
Each leaf a secret, each stem a jest,
In my cozy room, they are the best.

A pot or two may go 'pop'!
But laughter's the best flower shop.
With every corner, life sneaks in,
What a riot, this green-sprouted spin!

## **Layered Greens of Comfort**

In corners where the sunlight rests,
My leafy friends host tiny fests.
Each pot a world, a little tale,
Of growth, of whimsy, never stale.

A spider plant sent me a note,
Said, "Hey, don't forget to water, quote!"
While succulents argue on the shelf,
'You watered me more than yourself!'

A snake plant tiptoes, oh so sly,
Plotting its takeover; oh my, oh my!
With each green layer, mischief's born,
I'm just here sipping tea, forlorn.

Together we're a humorous crew,
Reading the best of plant humor, too.
In our indoor oasis of glee,
Life grows funnier by the cup, you see!

## Palette of Indoor Vibrance

In pots of colors bright and bold,
My indoor garden stories unfold.
Petunias laugh, while roses pout,
Sprinkling joy without a doubt.

A violet dreams of a big stage,
Performing nightly, turning the page.
While my basil tries to take the lead,
Saying, "Cook with me or you'll concede!"

The cheerful daisies play charades,
While ferns gossip about the parades.
Every corner's a gallery of schemes,
In this merry quilt of leafy dreams.

So here in my vibrant little space,
Life's a party at a steady pace.
With laughter, color, and cheeky delight,
My home's an art show both day and night.

## Sprout in Soft Light

In a corner, a plant stands tall,
Wearing sunlight like a shawl.
Whispers to the cat with a wink,
"Betcha can't outgrow me, you think?"

Sipping water, a little too much,
Leaves dance wildly, a soft touch.
The cactus laughs, all prickly pride,
"I'm the one with style, not just my side!"

Petals gossip, softly coo,
"Which one of us is the cutest, boo?"
Fern rolls over, charmingly shy,
"I've got fronds to flaunt, oh my!"

Potted pals share a gleeful cheer,
While the tulip strikes a jazzy sphere.
With each giggle, they brightened the room,
Nature's party, all ready to bloom!

## Secret Garden by the Hearth

A little pot holds secrets tight,
Dance of shadows in morning light.
The herbs all chat in fragrant thrill,
"Who knew we could spice up the chill?"

Nestled near the roaring flame,
The basil teases, it's all a game.
"Watch me save the dinner with flair!"
Sage replies, "I'm the one with rare air!"

Petunias giggle as they sway,
"Let's throw a bash for spring today!"
The thyme's got tunes, with zest to share,
Even the rosemary joins the fair!

Secrecy blooms in joyous glee,
By the hearth, let thoughts roam free!
With each laugh, the warmth descends,
In this cozy nook, joy never ends!

## Lively Leaves

Birch seems bored, it's quite a plight,
While ferns are giggling, all's just right.
"I'm losing my color, oh what a shame!"
The ivy mocks, "You're just feeling lame!"

Sprouts in a row have formed a band,
Walter the cabbage gives a hand.
"Let's sing a tune about the sun,
And show those pots how to have fun!"

The bellowing cabbage, with voice so loud,
Leaves pop and twist, they draw a crowd.
"Lively leaves, let's leap and twirl,
The plant party's on, come join our whirl!"

Soon the room echoes with their cheer,
Even our dog wants to draw near.
There's never a dull light when they thrive,
In their vibrant world, they come alive!

# Gentle Touches

A succulent winks in its cozy spot,
"Hey there friend, have you tried my plot?"
"Join my leaf dance, it's quite divine!
We'll make the dust bunnies twist and shine!"

Little buds sway like whispering dreams,
Sharing jokes with sunlight beams.
"Careful with that watering can, dude!
Too much love can break this mood!"

Leaves curl back when a shadow looms,
"Not too close now, we need some room!"
Sunflowers chuckle, "Ooh, what a spat!
Who knew plants could be such a brat?"

Giggles of greens fill the air bright,
With wild banter till the night!
Flora laughs, life takes its course,
While gentle touches brew a gentle force!

## **Serenity in a Terrarium**

In a glass globe, the peace resides,
Sassy moss and sprightly strides.
"Watch out, don't bump the fairy light!"
The air plants say with a quirky bite.

Gnomes in the corner, all dressed in cheer,
They throw a party for those who are near.
"Acts of kindness must fill this space,
Like sprinkles of joy in this tiny place!"

Each plant seems to giggle and sway,
"Can you believe we're in this play?
With little moments making us whole,
We create magic, that's our goal!"

The clock ticks slow, but joy is fast,
In this quiet space, pure fun is cast.
So gather round if you want to stay,
In this world of green, let's laugh away!

**Cozy Corners**

In the corner sits a pot,
With soil that's never hot.
Laughter echoes, leaves a-clatter,
As my cactus shrieks, 'What's the matter?'

Dust bunnies dance on windowsills,
While my fern just drinks its thrills.
They throw a party, no one tells,
Except the spider who just yells!

## **Leafy Friends**

Two ferns gossip, green and bright,
Complaining 'bout the lack of light.
'I'm not a llama, I'm not a cow,'
Says one to the other, 'But who cares now?'

The pothos sings a song off-key,
While wandering vines play hide and seek.
In this jungle, giggles grow,
As on each leaf, the sunshine glows.

## Tapestry of Indoor Blooms

In hues of pink and yellow cheer,
My flowers dance, oh dear, oh dear!
They sway and giggle, sprouting rhymes,
Like poets caught in silly crimes.

A daisy winks, the violets sneeze,
While tulips gossip in the breeze.
In this tapestry so grand,
I'm the leaf, they're the band!

## Secret Lives of Houseplants

When I sleep, the leaves confide,
In secret whispers, they can't hide.
'Who knew the philodendron could dance?'
Says the succulent, 'I had a chance!'

Potting soil spills, pests try to creep,
But the plants are smart and they don't weep.
With their roots entwined, they plot and scheme,
For world domination, or so it seems!

## Chlorophyll Dreams

In dreamland where the green things play,
A leafy llama leads the way.
Sipping sunlight from a cup,
The houseplants giggle as they sup.

With chlorophyll as their grand attire,
They jump and frolic in green desire.
With dreams of dirt and dances bold,
They're living stories yet untold.

## Green Sanctuary Beneath the Roof

In a pot sits a cactus, spiky and bold,
Telling tales of deserts, or so I'm told.
I water it gently, though it looks quite fine,
It just rolls its eyes, makes me question my time.

A fern in the corner, as green as can be,
Waving its fronds like it's hosting a spree.
I whisper sweet nothings, it leans in for fun,
As if it could hear me, oh what have I done?

Daisies on windowsills, petals aflutter,
Noticing the sun, it's like they just shudder.
"Is this daylight savings? My petals are warm!"
"I'd rather be outside, not stuck in this form!"

Beneath the roof lies a jungle of cheer,
Where plant life presides, nothing quite to fear.
They laugh and they giggle, in their leafy brigade,
Creating a wonderland, my own leafy parade.

## Nature's Vignette Indoors

A succulent sits proud, in the light of the day,
Turns its little head, 'What's for dinner, okay?'
Smooth and content, it sips water with grace,
While I bring home takeout, it claims my space.

The spider plant swings, oh what a wild ride,
"Be careful!" I warn, "Don't slip on that slide!"
"Your kids are multiplying!" I say with a grin,
"You're running a nursery and I'm just chipping in!"

A rubber tree gossiping with ferns and peace lilies,
Sharing the scoop of my clumsy, wild frillies.
"Who watered the thyme? It's wilting, I hear!"
They chuckle so loudly; goodness, their roots cheer!

In this indoor tableau, where laughter takes flight,
Nature's own sitcom, a bit of delight.
I dance in the warmth, as their stories unfold,
In pots full of laughter, these memories hold.

## Potted Reveries

A violet peeks out, with a curious grin,
"Did you bring any snacks, or just your own skin?"
I chuckle aloud, as it sways to the beat,
My little plant party, a gathering sweet.

A tiny basil waits, with its leafy flair,
Plotting a pesto he'd like to declare.
"I'm ready, my friend, just grab that food chopper!
Soon we'll be blending and I'll be a showstopper!"

The jade plant watches, wise as can be,
"Meditate daily, my friend—honestly!
Life in a pot can be quite a delight,
Unless you're the one whose turn's to be light!"

In the kitchen we gather, a potted crew,
Filling the air with laughter so true.
These quirky companions, they brighten my days,
In this pot-laden world, where greenery plays.

## The Indoor Herbarium


Thyme and rosemary, friends on the shelf,
Arguing softly; both claiming their health.
"Not too much sunlight!" thyme yells with a squeak,
While rosemary smirks, "You'll sway to the peak!"

The chives are on strike, with their heads held high,
"Cut me some slack and I might not die!"
I giggle imagining their leafy debates,
As herbs share their tales of marvelous fates.

A pot full of mint is the life of the show,
"Just make me a mojito, and watch me glow!"
I roll my eyes, this indoor bazaar,
Where flavors collide, it's just too bizarre!

Some say a green thumb is all I require,
But I just bring puns to the plant-filled choir.
Together we laugh, in this quirky domain,
Living our lives like a botanical chain.

# The Enchanted Corner

In the nook a fern does dance,
With a jaunty little prance.
The cat thinks it's his new friend,
On mischief, he's set to spend.

Potted herbs with scents so bold,
In the sunlight, stories told.
A basil thief, green and sly,
Nibbles leaves while I sigh.

Cacti wear tiny hats of blue,
Pretend they're tough, but they aren't true.
They stand sentry, oh so proud,
While I'm laughing, loud and loud.

In this jungle, chaos reigned,
Yet with flowers, I'm un-chained.
Funny antics, plants go wild,
In this world, I'm a child.

## Nature's Canvas Indoors

Painted petals, colors bright,
Regal blooms give pure delight.
Driftwood vines, they twist and twine,
In this gallery, I'm divine!

A pot of daisies up on high,
Tries to hypnotize the fly.
While my dog, he takes a leap,
To snag that fly, and then he sleeps.

Succulents are fashion models,
Strutting in their spiky throttles.
"Look at me," they seem to say,
"I'm the trend of the day!"

But then a spider took the stage,
Wove a web, unleashed a rage.
Nature's mad, but who would know,
Indoor life's a wild show!

## Still Life in Green

A single leaf with a funny frown,
Mocks the rosy blooms in the town.
"I'm all alone, so sad and meek,"
But with a twist, it starts to speak!

The orchids in their fancy dress,
Hold a dance, what a mess!
They tangle up and fall with flair,
Please call for help, they need repair!

Chive whispers secrets of the night,
While thyme taps its tiny feet in fright.
"Oh dear," they giggle, "what a sight!"
Their tiny drama brings pure delight.

In this staging of my dreams,
Laughter rustles, or so it seems.
Pom-poms of petals in a row,
With each chuckle, they surely grow!

## Harmony of Indoor Blooms


Peonies plot behind the vase,
With witty grins, they play their case.
"Let's throw a party!" they decide,
With potted friends all gathered wide.

Petunias gossip in the sun,
They wager bets on who will run.
Lilies chuckle, show their might,
With petals bright, they take to flight.

A rogue spider drops in late,
Claims his place amidst the fate.
"Don't mind me," he gives a wink,
With charm, he steals their drink!

But every plant agrees it's fun,
With nature's art we've just begun.
In this room, the laughter blooms,
Where silence, it just couldn't loom.

www.ingramcontent.com/pod-product-compliance
Lightning Source LLC
Chambersburg PA
CBHW050306120526
44590CB00016B/2513